THE
COLORADO
TRAIL
Databook

FOURTH EDITION

THE COLORADO TRAIL
FOUNDATION

The Colorado Mountain Club Press
Golden, Colorado

The Colorado Trail Databook: A CMC Pack Guide
© 2009 The Colorado Mountain Club

7/2012

PUBLISHED BY

The Colorado Mountain Club Press
710 Tenth Street, Suite 200, Golden, Colorado 80401
303-996-2743   e-mail: cmcpress@cmc.org

CMC Press Publisher: Alan Stark
Graphics Design and Maps: Valerie Z. Miller and Terry Root
The Colorado Trail Foundation, project volunteer, surveyor, and cartographer:
    Jerry Brown
Fourth Edition GPS data © 2009, Jerry Brown, Bear Creek Survey Service,
    www.bearcreeksurvey.com
Front cover photo: On the CT in the quaking aspens, courtesy Colorado Mountain
    Expeditions

DISTRIBUTED TO THE BOOK TRADE BY
Mountaineers Books, 1001 SW Klickitat Way, Suite 201, Seattle, WA 98134,
800-553-4453, www.mountaineerbooks.org

We gratefully acknowledge the financial support of the people of
Colorado through the Scientific and Cultural Facilities District of
greater metropolitan Denver for our publishing activities.

Second Printing

ISBN 978-0-9799663-7-8

Printed in the United States of America

Warning: Although there has been a major effort to make the information in this book as accurate as possible, some discrepancies may exist between the text and the lay of the trail in the field. Therefore, extreme care should be taken when following any of the routes described in this book. This book is not intended to be instructional in nature but rather a guide for users of The Colorado Trail who already have the requisite training, experience and knowledge. In addition, there may be differences in the way certain individuals interpret the information beyond that intended. Before you begin an extended trek, or even a short hike, on The Colorado Trail, all users need to be fully capable of independent backcountry mountaineering and orienteering techniques and precautions. Proper clothing and equipment are essential. Failure to have the necessary knowledge, equipment and conditioning will subject users of The Colorado Trail to extreme physical danger, injury or death. Each user of The Colorado Trail is responsible and liable for all costs which may be incurred if a rescue is necessary.

WELCOME TO THE COLORADO TRAIL®

The Colorado Trail (CT) is a premier, high mountain recreation trail nearly 500 miles long across the Rocky Mountains from Denver to Durango. The CT passes through five national forests and six wilderness areas, traverses five major river systems and penetrates eight of the state's mountain ranges. The CT was created by volunteers and has an impressive history.

Conceived in 1973 by a partnership of the US Forest Service and private sector, the CT was connected end-to-end in 1987. It continues to be maintained by volunteers organized by The Colorado Trail Foundation (CTF), the nonprofit organization that built the trail. The CTF takes great pride in preserving The Colorado Trail for everyone and, if you'd like to help volunteer or support the effort, please visit **www.ColoradoTrail.org**.

The acknowledged bible for day-hikers, backpackers, cyclists and horse riders exploring the CT is *The Colorado Trail, Seventh Edition Revised*, referred to as the Guidebook in this text. The 256-page guidebook provides all the information needed for planning a trip on the CT, including detailed access directions, mile-by-mile descriptions, information on re-supply points, full-color maps, background on history and natural features, dozens of full-color photographs and much more.

The *Colorado Trail Databook* was developed for trail users to easily carry in pocket or pack. It provides a reference to major features on the CT and is designed to answer common, on-the-trail questions such as: Where's the next water? How many miles have I gone? Where am I camping tonight? Where's the next re-supply?

The Databook includes the work of several CTF volunteers, led most recently by volunteer surveyor and cartographer, Jerry Brown. As each edition incorporates data from previous editions, it is impossible to ensure the absolute accuracy of this information. Also noteworthy is that the CT changes every year. Portions are rerouted, access changes with fires and floods, and closures occur on private property. Users should check the CTF website, **www.ColoradoTrail.org**, for trail changes before venturing out on the CT. If you have suggestions for future editions of the Databook, such as new campsites or additional water sources, please contact us at:

The Colorado Trail Foundation
Email: CTF@ColoradoTrail.org   Phone: 303-384-3729
Mail: 710 10th Street #210, Golden, CO 80401

USING THE DATABOOK

The CT is described in 28 segments and each represents a chapter in the Databook. The map on page 7 shows the entire 485-mile trail as well as the major access roads. The Databook is presented from the vantage point of one traveling east to west on the CT, as most do. "East" and "West" refers to the general direction of travel, that is, from Denver to Durango, regardless of the fact that individual segments of the CT may run north/south. Therefore, one traveling from west to east would do the opposite that the book indicates and "turn left" where the book indicates "turn right."

Each chapter includes a **data chart** on the left page with segment summary info in the heading. The elevation gain is the sum of major ascending portions and a general indicator of how much effort will be required. At top-right is a book icon that shows corresponding page numbers within the bigger Guidebook.

The main body of the data chart presents waypoints of significant features encountered along that segment; including trailheads, intersections with other trails or roads, stream crossings, wilderness boundaries, directional changes, water sources, campsites, and places of special interest, such as viewpoints or historical sites. Numbers in the left column under "THe" are the mileages from the eastern trailhead of that segment. Numbers in the right column under "THw" are the mileages from the western trailhead. To determine total accumulated mileage from either the Denver end of the CT or the Durango end, add these numbers to mileages in the **segment distance chart** on page 7.

Each mileage entry includes a descriptive phrase, approximate elevation, plus waypoint data in UTM (NAD 83). UTM is a rectangular, straight-line system of x-y coordinates, not unlike a checkerboard. Many trail users report it to be the easiest system to use and that it makes more sense than trying to decipher latitude-longitude pairs. Most trail maps now show UTM, enabling trail users to pinpoint their position on the map using the UTM coordinates in the Databook. GPS users can manually enter a UTM coordinate and verify where they are. Using simple subtraction, GPS users can learn they are a certain number of meters away from a desired location. Be certain to follow the instructions for your particular GPS manufacturer. **Before entering UTM data into the GPS unit,** set the GPS position format to UTM/UPS and set the datum (may be called spheroid) to either NAD83 or WGS84. Once the UTM waypoint has been entered, if desired, GPS users can easily convert to Lat-Long by switching the coordinate format. Waypoint users need to be aware that the UTM zone switches in Segment 27 (see data chart) from UTM Zone 13 to Zone 12 at the 108-degree longitude line. It returns to Zone 13 early in Segment 28. Most GPS receivers will make this transition automatically when you cross the line. If for some reason your GPS doesn't, turning it off then on again will usually do the trick.

At the bottom of the waypoint pages, an **elevation profile** shows the major climbs and descents in that segment and also shows the relative steepness of portions of the trail. The bottom scale shows mileage from the eastern trailhead and the top scale shows mileage from the western trailhead.

On the page opposite the data chart is the **mini-map** for that segment, with distances to scale and showing, by means of graphic symbols, the location of most of the features for that segment. **Bold** mileage numbers identify points that are displayed on the mini-map. The map also shows alternate trailheads, important roads and some stream courses. Nearby supply points and services are listed, with symbols indicating what types of services are available. Towns or supply points with post offices that accept general delivery are indicated with their zip code. However, note that for some remote segments of the CT, no convenient points of supply are available.

SAFETY ON THE COLORADO TRAIL

An experienced hiker will be prepared and take no unnecessary chances. Along the more isolated portions of the CT, assistance will be many hours, even days, away. The Colorado Trail Foundation strongly recommends that you purchase a *Colorado Outdoor Recreation Search and Rescue* (CORSAR) card (web search term CORSAR). To activate a rescue group, contact the nearest county sheriff. Travelers on The Colorado Trail should keep the following points in mind:

Beware of the conditions. The varied terrain of The Colorado Trail puts you at risk for both hypothermia and dehydration. Plan for the possibility of each, as well as the lightning hazard of exposed ridges.

Start hiking early. You will encounter storms of varying intensity, whether midsummer thunderstorms or late summer snow showers. An early start gives generally clear mornings and plenty of time to set up camp at your day's end.

Travel with a companion. Backpacking or hiking alone is not recommended, even for the experienced. If you do so, make sure your itinerary is known by others and check in as often as possible.

Be in shape. Your best insurance against accidents is to be in top physical condition. Acclimatize yourself before beginning your trek, and guard against fatigue. Pushing yourself too hard in rugged terrain can be disastrous.

Be prepared. Put together an equipment list, such as that on page 20 of the Guidebook. Be prepared to purify all drinking water by boiling, by applying disinfectant or by filtering. Have a basic first-aid kit and know how to use it. Have maps of your intended route and be aware of rules and regulations that apply. Be alert for the CT symbol on signs along the way. Enjoy your excursion on The Colorado Trail.

Segment	County Sheriff	
1–3	Jefferson	(303) 277-0211
4–6	Park	(719) 836-2494
6–8	Summit	(970) 453-2232
8	Eagle	(970) 328-8500
9–11	Lake	(719) 486-1249
12–15	Chaffee	(719) 539-2814
15–20	Saguache	(719) 655-2544
21	Mineral	(719) 658-2600
21–23	Hinsdale	(970) 944-2291
24–25	San Juan	(970) 387-5531
26	Dolores	(970) 677-2257
27–28	La Plata	(970) 247-1157

SYMBOLS USED IN THE DATABOOK

11.1 Mileage calculated from the eastern trailhead of the segment (*THe*).

THe Eastern trailhead or terminus of the segment.

THw Western trailhead or terminus of the segment.

Paved or graded-dirt access road, suitable for any vehicle.

Rough dirt access road but suitable for most vehicles in dry conditions.

4-wheel-drive access road or impassable in very wet conditions.

Segment involves no Wilderness Area and is suitable for mountain bikes.

Segment involves terrain challenging to bicyclists and a detour is recommended, but not required. See Guidebook for bicycle detours.

Segment involves Wilderness Area where mountain bikes are prohibited. See Guidebook for bicycle detours.

The CT intersects a road or another trail, either marked or unmarked. Users should be alert to any changes in direction.

The CT crosses a stream course, either dry or flowing. There may be a bridge or it may necessitate a ford.

Previously established campsite is nearby. New campsites should only be established if necessary, according to the regulations in force.

Water source, such as a spring, lake or creek, reliable in most years.

Water source, such as a spring, lake or creek, with only seasonal flow.

Water source, such as a spring, lake or creek, scarce or unreliable.

Place of special interest, such as a viewpoint or historical site.

70 Major state or federal highway.

91 Secondary road which may or may not be paved.

Services at supply points

Post Office · Lodging · Meals · Groceries · Telephone · Bank · Showers · Camp Gear · Laundry · Medical

58 63 Corresponding page numbers from the Guidebook

ABBREVIATIONS USED
C = campsite
TH = trailhead
CG = campground
W = water   w/ = with
cr = creek   m = mile

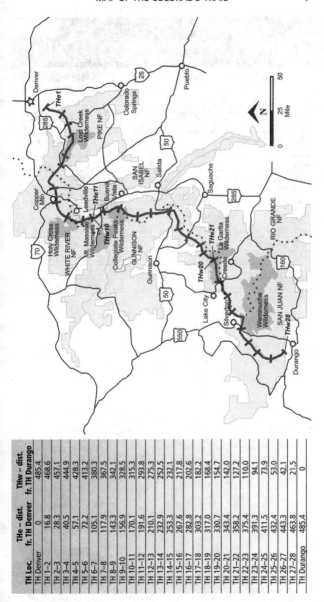

TH Loc.	THe – dist. fr. TH Denver	THw – dist. fr. TH Durango
TH Denver	0	485.4
TH 1–2	16.8	468.6
TH 2–3	28.3	457.1
TH 3–4	40.5	444.9
TH 4–5	57.1	428.3
TH 5–6	72.2	413.2
TH 6–7	105.1	380.3
TH 7–8	117.9	367.5
TH 8–9	143.3	342.1
TH 9–10	156.9	328.5
TH 10–11	170.1	315.3
TH 11–12	191.6	293.8
TH 12–13	210.1	275.3
TH 13–14	232.9	252.5
TH 14–15	253.3	232.1
TH 15–16	267.6	217.8
TH 16–17	282.8	202.6
TH 17–18	303.2	182.2
TH 18–19	317.0	168.4
TH 19–20	330.7	154.7
TH 20–21	343.4	142.0
TH 21–22	358.2	127.2
TH 22–23	375.4	110.0
TH 23–24	391.3	94.1
TH 24–25	411.5	73.9
TH 25–26	432.4	53.0
TH 26–27	443.3	42.1
TH 27–28	463.8	21.5
TH Durango	485.4	0

SEGMENT 1
Kassler to South Platte Canyon
Distance: 16.8 miles   Elevation Gain: approx 2160 ft

THe	Feature	Elevation	UTM (NAD 83)	THw
0.0	Waterton Canyon TH, no C allowed for next 6.2m, W at many spots along the river	5520	491,827E 4,371,302N Z13	16.8
6.2	pass Strontia Springs Dam, leave river	5800	489,428E 4,365,023N Z13	10.6
6.7	begin single track	5920	489,711E 4,364,357N Z13	10.1
7.0	small C on left w/no W, 100 feet before start of switchbacks	6180		9.8
7.9	Lenny's Rest/pass trail to Carpenter Pk	6560	489,598E 4,363,840N Z13	8.9
8.7	cross Bear Cr, C 100' before, on right (last reliable W for 8.0m)	6200	489,297E 4,363,337N Z13	8.1
9.6	join Motorcycle Trail #692 for 0.5m	6640	489,178E 4,362,657N Z13	7.2
9.8	parallel, then cross West Bear Creek	6760	489,063E 4,362,460N Z13	7.0
10.2	diverge from motorcycle trail	6900	488,822E 4,362,057N Z13	6.6
10.8	motorcycle trail crosses CT final time	7200	488,452E 4,362,417N Z13	5.8
11.8	C, w/no W at leaning rocks	7300	487,539E 4,362,374N Z13	4.8
12.6	high point on ridge	7520	486,841E 4,361,820N Z13	4.2
16.8	South Platte Canyon	6120	485,565E 4,361,212N Z13	0.0

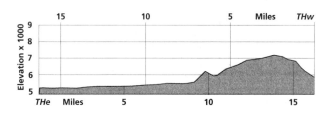

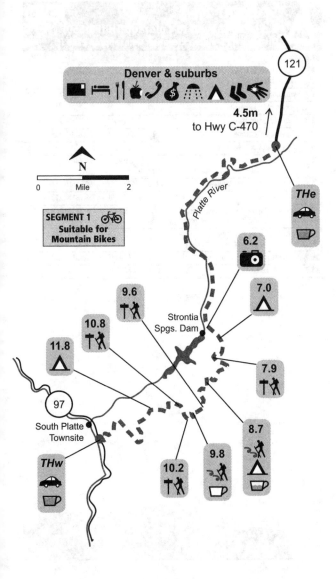

SEGMENT 2
S. Platte Canyon to Colorado TH (FS-550)
Distance: 11.5 miles   Elevation Gain: approx 2200 ft

`54` `59`

THe	Feature	Elevation	UTM (NAD 83)		THw
0.0	South Platte Canyon (last reliable W for 13.0m)	6120	485,565E 4,361,212N	Z13	11.5
0.1	wrap under bridge	6100	485,514E 4,361,190N	Z13	11.4
1.1	pick up old quarry road	6600	485,160E 4,360,758N	Z13	10.4
1.3	leave old quarry road	6760	484,901E 4,360,725N	Z13	10.3
2.5	large granite outcrop	7120	483,612E 4,361,244N	Z13	9.0
5.2	ridge, Chair Rocks visible to west	7760	480,693E 4,361,700N	Z13	6.3
6.0	meet FS-538 at 3-corner intersection, cross and go south parallel to road	7760	479,996E 4,361,244N	Z13	5.5
6.6	C off side trail to left, w/no W	7760	479,674E 4,360,515N	Z13	4.9
7.3	cross jeep road	7620	479,319E 4,359,731N	Z13	4.2
10.0	meet Cty Rd-126/Spring Creek Road, go south parallel to highway (emergency W at firehouse, north along road)	7600	478,845E 4,356,741N	Z13	1.5
10.5	cross to west side of highway, go west along Forest Service road	7650	478,666E 4,356,299N	Z13	1.0
10.7	C, where road turns south	7600	478,414E 4,356,401N	Z13	0.8
11.5	Colorado TH on FS-550	7840	477,783E 4,355,124N	Z13	0.0

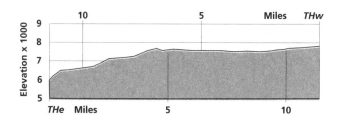

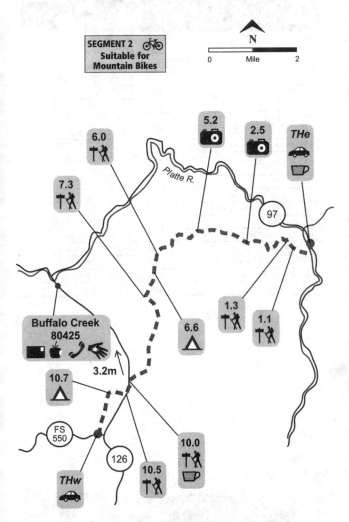

SEGMENT 3
Colorado TH (FS-550) to FS-560
Distance: 12.2 miles   Elevation Gain: approx 1520 ft

THe	Feature	Elevation	UTM (NAD 83)	THw
0.0	Colorado TH on FS-550	7840	477,783E 4,355,124N Z13	12.2
0.6	cross FS-550	7840	477,117E 4,354,829N Z13	11.6
1.7	C w/no W	7800	475,789E 4,354,677N Z13	10.5
1.9	cross Shinglemill bicycle trail	7780	475,591E 4,354,778N Z13	10.3
2.8	bear to right, cross creek	7760	475,402E 4,353,638N Z13	9.4
4.5	join and descend an old road	8000	474,484E 4,353,069N Z13	7.7
5.1	cross Tramway Creek	7600	473,709E 4,353,530N Z13	7.1
5.6	take sharp left at Tramway bicycle trail	7680	473,322E 4,353,875N Z13	6.6
6.3	take right fork at Green Mountain bicycle trail	7600	472,598E 4,353,856N Z13	5.9
7.0	side trail goes right to Buffalo CG	7540	471,694E 4,354,181N Z13	5.2
7.5	cross old logging road	7560	471,187E 4,354,505N Z13	4.7
7.6	cutoff for Meadows Group CG	7400	470,946E 4,354,572N Z13	4.6
7.7	pass gate	7380	470,808E 4,354,595N Z13	4.5
8.0	cross FS-543 and Buffalo Creek	7400	470,682E 4,354,577N Z13	4.2
9.1	C w/no W	7900	469,228E 4,354,718N Z13	3.1
9.6	cross Buffalo Creek Gun Club Road	7920	468,473E 4,354,753N Z13	2.6
11.9	cross small stream	8160	465,855E 4,354,444N Z13	0.3
12.2	FS-560	8280	465,429E 4,354,406N Z13	0.0

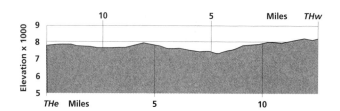

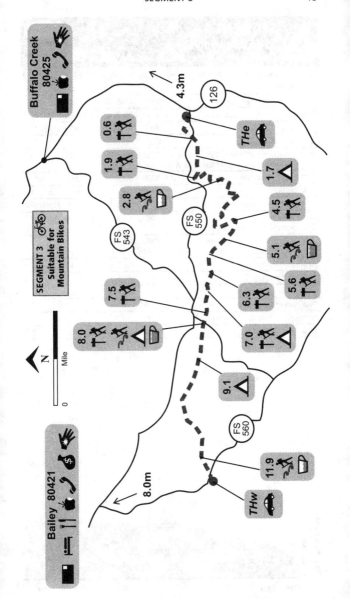

SEGMENT 4
FS-560 to Long Gulch
Distance: 16.6 miles   Elevation Gain: approx 2840 ft

`66` `73`

THe	Feature	Elevation	UTM (NAD 83)		THw
0.0	FS-560	8280	465,429E 4,354,406N	Z13	16.6
0.3	leave road, CT goes to right	8360	465,294E 4,354,122N	Z13	16.3
1.0	join old road, goes southwest	8560	464,474E 4,354,588N	Z13	15.7
1.9	wilderness boundary	9100	463,618E 4,353,766N	Z13	14.7
2.4	seasonal stream	9200	463,026E 4,353,592N	Z13	14.2
3.3	take left fork at Payne Cr Trail junction, C 50 yards down the right fork, w/no W	9320	461,803E 4,353,395N	Z13	13.3
4.5	cross small stream	9360	460,491E 4,352,265N	Z13	12.1
5.6	leave old road to left	9840	459,175E 4,351,669N	Z13	11.0
7.4	rejoin old road on forested ridge	10460	457,542E 4,350,771N	Z13	9.2
8.2	cross North Fork of Lost Creek, cross wilderness boundary	10280	456,422E 4,351,041N	Z13	8.4
8.9	cross Brookside-McCurdy Trail (left on Brookside-McCurdy for Lost Park CG and TH, 1.7m w/C and W)	10200	455,590E 4,350,933N	Z13	7.7
9.2	cross tributary stream	10240	455,326E 4,351,281N	Z13	7.4
11.3	cross tributary stream	10400	452,524E 4,352,903N	Z13	5.1
14.5	saddle at head of N. Fork, C w/no W	10880	448,413E 4,355,450N	Z13	2.1
14.6	turn south, views from outcrops	10800			2.0
16.5	cross stream, spur trail down to TH	10200			0.1
16.6	Long Gulch	10160	446,882E 4,355,620N	Z13	0.0

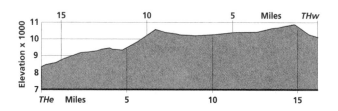

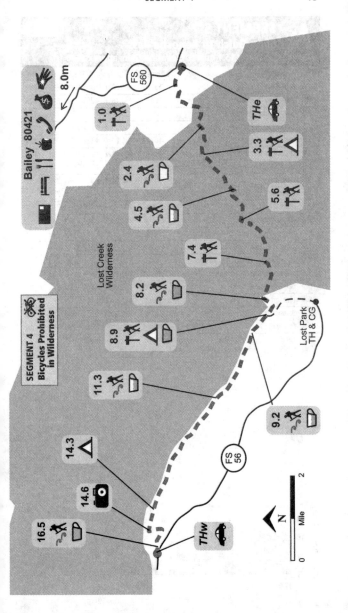

SEGMENT 5
Long Gulch to Kenosha Pass
Distance: 15.1 miles   Elevation Gain: approx 1540 ft

[74] [79]

THe	Feature	Elevation	UTM (NAD 83)	THw
0.0	Long Gulch	10160	446,882E 4,355,620N Z13	15.1
0.3	wilderness boundary	10220	446,494E 4,355,578N Z13	14.8
2.2	gain saddle	10520		13.0
2.9	cross seasonal stream	10370	445,292E 4,357,257N Z13	12.2
3.1	cross marshy area	10380	445,247E 4,357,475N Z13	12.0
3.9	cross seasonal stream	10320	444,712E 4,358,504N Z13	11.2
4.5	cross seasonal stream	10220	444,333E 4,358,566N Z13	10.6
5.3	cross creek	10160	443,443E 4,359,029N Z13	9.8
6.6	wilderness boundary	9800	441,738E 4,357,965N Z13	8.5
7.3	cross Rock Creek	9520	441,104E 4,357,452N Z13	7.8
7.4	intersect Ben Tyler Trail	9540	441,079E 4,357,404N Z13	7.7
7.6	pass red gate, turn right on old road	9580	441,333E 4,357,157N Z13	7.5
7.8	leave road, trail resumes on left	9710	440,785E 4,357,218N Z13	7.3
8.0	cross FS-133 at Rock Creek TH	9720	440,776E 4,357,207N Z13	7.1
8.4	cross seasonal stream/Johnson Gulch	9520	440,261E 4,357,095N Z13	6.7
10.0	panorama point w/views	10000	437,979E 4,358,230N Z13	5.1
11.4	turn left on jeep road	10200	437,381E 4,359,835N Z13	3.7
13.2	defunct irrigation channel	10240	436,426E 4,361,295N Z13	1.9
14.9	follow road to SW	10080	435,018E 4,362,945N Z13	0.2
15.1	Kenosha Pass/US Hwy-285, C w/W in campground on west side of highway	10000	434,724E 4,362,829N Z13	0.0

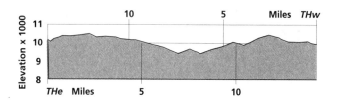

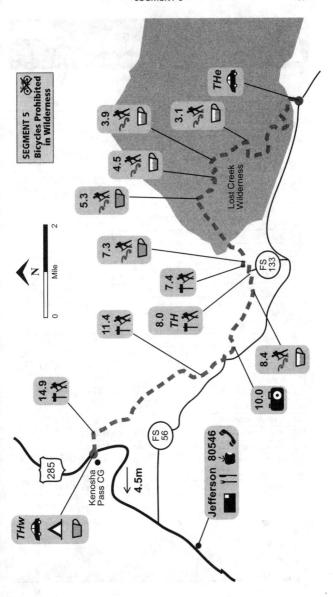

SEGMENT 6
Kenosha Pass to Goldhill Trailhead
Distance: 32.9 miles   Elevation Gain: approx 4520 ft

| 80 | 87 |

THe	Feature	Elevation	UTM (NAD 83)	THw
0.0	Kenosha Pass/US Hwy-285	10000	434,724E 4,362,829N Z13	32.9
1.5	cross old road	10280	432,603E 4,363,668N Z13	31.4
3.0	cross FS-809	9880	431,008E 4,364,547N Z13	29.9
3.1	pass over Guernsey Creek on log	9880	430,950E 4,364,524N Z13	29.8
4.4	cross FS-427	10100	428,883E 4,364,683N Z13	28.5
4.5	cross Deadman Creek	10100	428,671E 4,364,711N Z13	28.4
4.9	go right onto old jeep road	10160	428,069E 4,364,828N Z13	28.0
5.0	cross small stream, trail resumes left	10180	428,095E 4,364,805N Z13	27.9
5.2	gain saddle, pass gate	10200	428,143E 4,364,439N Z13	27.7
5.9	cross Jefferson Lake Road	10000	427,277E 4,364,791N Z13	27.0
6.0	cross Jefferson Creek on bridge	10000	427,198E 4,364,680N Z13	26.9
6.1	go right on intersecting trail	10000	427,051E 4,364,626N Z13	26.8
6.2	go left at fork	10020	426,967E 4,364,744N Z13	26.7
7.8	cross side trail to Michigan Cr Road	10680	425,237E 4,364,884N Z13	25.1
11.7	cross Jefferson Cr Trail, W 0.3m north	11600	422,370E 4,367,556N Z13	21.8
12.1	cross jeep track	11820	421,847E 4,367,858N Z13	20.8
12.3	gain Continental Divide (Continental Divide Trail co-located with CT next 99m to Twin Lakes)	11860	421,619E 4,367,998N Z13	20.6
12.5	cross Glacier Ridge Rd, go right	11800	421,696E 4,368,342N Z13	20.4
15.4	cross old road	10960	420,857E 4,370,885N Z13	17.5
17.1	go right for 50 ft. on Middle Fork Road	10160	420,411E 4,372,426N Z13	15.8
19.7	cross N. Fork Swan River, cross road	10000	419,661E 4,374,519N Z13	13.2
20.1	go right, parallel seasonal stream	10200	419,339E 4,374,809N Z13	12.8
22.2	trail levels out on ridge	11040	419,177E 4,376,814N Z13	10.7
22.6	go left as trail forks	11000	418,778E 4,377,279N Z13	10.3
23.8	go left at another fork	10860	417,675E 4,378,355N Z13	9.1
26.1	go left at T-road, C w/W 0.2 back	10000	416,521E 4,377,391N Z13	6.8
27.5	go right at fork in lodgepole forest	9880	415,356E 4,377,124N Z13	5.4
28.8	cross Horseshoe Gulch, C 0.2m after	9400	414,089E 4,376,884N Z13	4.1
32.4	cross Hwy-9, go right on bike path	9200	410,431E 4,377,005N Z13	0.5
32.9	Goldhill TH	9200	410,455E 4,377,354N Z13	0.0

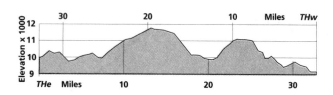

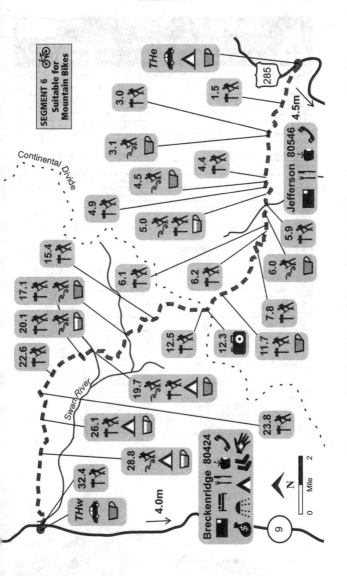

SEGMENT 7
Goldhill Trailhead to Copper Mountain
Distance: 12.8 miles   Elevation Gain: approx 3600 ft

THe	Feature	Elevation	UTM (NAD 83)		THw
0.0	Hwy-9, Goldhill TH	9200	410,455E 4,377,354N	Z13	12.8
0.2	C, w/W 0.2m east at Goldhill TH	9300	410,256E 4,377,234N	Z13	12.6
1.0	3-way logging road intersection, go left	9660	409,065E 4,377,498N	Z13	11.8
1.6	cross logging road	9960	408,702E 4,376,653N	Z13	11.2
2.0	intersect old road, go right (north)	10120	408,383E 4,376,950N	Z13	10.8
2.3	rounded, rocky summit	10240	408,041E 4,377,044N	Z13	10.5
3.2	C, w/W	10020	407,022E 4,376,995N	Z13	9.6
3.4	join Peaks Trail (coincide for 0.3m)	9920	407,119E 4,376,553N	Z13	9.4
3.5	cross Miners Creek tributary	9960	406,982E 4,376,573N	Z13	9.3
3.9	re-cross Miners Creek tributary	10000	406,445E 4,376,225N	Z13	8.9
4.0	re-cross & leave Miners Cr tributary	10280	406,402E 4,376,181N	Z13	8.8
4.3	C, w/ no W	10480	406,275E 4,376,349N	Z13	8.5
4.8	access point for Miners Cr jeep trail, C w/W 200 ft west at bridge over Miners Creek	10560	405,670E 4,376,507N	Z13	8.0
5.7	finger of alpine tundra	11080	404,830E 4,376,214N	Z13	7.1
6.1	cross small seasonal stream	11120	404,639E 4,375,825N	Z13	6.7
6.5	small saddle	11840	404,534E 4,375,260N	Z13	6.3
7.6	seasonal spring	12320	404,421E 4,373,758N	Z13	5.2
8.0	crest of Tenmile Range	12440	404,219E 4,373,364N	Z13	4.8
9.0	seasonal spring	12200	404,227E 4,371,865N	Z13	3.8
9.6	tree line	11640	404,055E 4,370,864N	Z13	3.2
10.4	join Wheeler Trail, W 0.1 south	11240	404,066E 4,370,149N	Z13	2.4
10.7	seasonal spring	10560	403,906E 4,370,395N	Z13	2.1
11.8	seasonal spring	10120	402,885E 4,371,874N	Z13	1.0
12.4	intersect jeep trail, go west across Tenmile Cr bridge, then left (south) along power line	9760	402,368E 4,372,579N	Z13	0.4
12.8	Hwy-91	9800	402,335E 4,372,046N	Z13	0.0

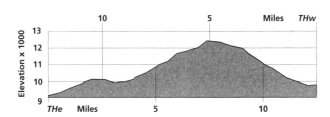

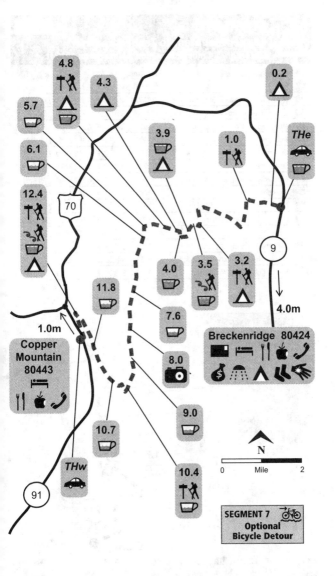

SEGMENT 8
Copper Mountain to Tennessee Pass
Distance: 25.4 miles   Elevation Gain: approx 4020 ft

96 103

THe	Feature	Elevation	UTM (NAD 83)		THw
0.0	Hwy-91	9800	402,335E 4,372,046N	Z13	25.4
1.7	cross stream, overlook Copper Mtn.	9760	400,721E 4,372,831N	Z13	23.7
5.2	Guller Creek, C .1m uphill on side tr.	10400	397,633E 4,371,608N	Z13	20.2
6.2	elongated meadow w/several good C	10600	396,349E 4,370,770N	Z13	19.2
8.7	tree line	11600	394,006E 4,369,297N	Z13	16.7
9.2	Guller Creek headwaters	11800	394,272E 4,368,761N	Z13	16.2
9.7	Searle Pass	12040	394,332E 4,368,348N	Z13	15.7
10.2	exposed C, W from snowmelt runoff	12000	394,220E 4,367,662N	Z13	15.2
12.4	Elk Ridge	12280	395,116E 4,365,436N	Z13	13.0
12.9	Kokomo Pass	12020	394,405E 4,365,068N	Z13	12.5
13.2	Cataract Creek headwaters	11800	394,186E 4,365,415N	Z13	12.2
13.5	tree line	11640	393,632E 4,365,845N	Z13	11.9
16.5	switchback left at jeep road crossing	10060	390,731E 4,364,642N	Z13	8.9
17.2	Cataract Falls, cross creek on bridge	9680	390,524E 4,364,435N	Z13	8.2
17.9	FS-714 (follow west for 800 ft.)	9400	389,339E 4,364,312N	Z13	7.5

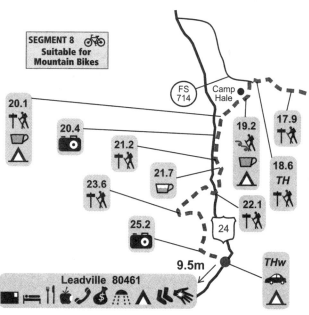

SEGMENT 8
Suitable for
Mountain Bikes

FS 714   Camp Hale

20.1

20.4

21.2

21.7

23.6

25.2

19.2

17.9

18.6 TH

22.1

24

9.5m

Leadville 80461

THw

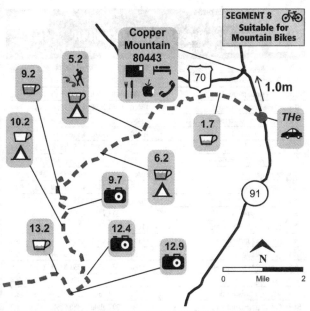

THe	Feature	Elevation	UTM (NAD 83)	THw
18.6	Camp Hale TH (W for 600 ft.then S)	9400	388,229E 4,364,653N Z13	6.8
19.2	cross bridge, C sw near bunkers	9320	387,892E 4,364,149N Z13	6.2
20.1	FS-226, C 0.1m north, W 0.2m north	9680	386,859E 4,363,442N Z13	5.3
20.4	bench and scenic overlook	9740	386,799E 4,363,011N Z13	5.0
21.2	cross jeep road	9880	386,601E 4,361,960N Z13	4.2
21.7	footbridge over Fiddler Creek	9940	386,751E 4,361,352N Z13	3.7
22.1	cross US Hwy-24	10000	386,556E 4,360,752N Z13	3.3
23.6	join jeep road	10200	385,625E 4,359,709N Z13	1.8
25.2	remains of coking ovens	10300	386,477E 4,358,073N Z13	0.2
25.4	Tennessee Pass/US Hwy-24	10424	386,983E 4,357,913N Z13	0.0

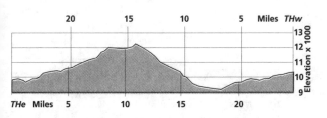

SEGMENT 9
Tennessee Pass to Colorado Trail TH
Distance: 13.6 miles   Elevation Gain: approx 2120 ft

`104` `109`

THe	Feature	Elevation	UTM (NAD 83)			THw
0.0	Tennessee Pass/US Hwy-24	10424	386,983E	4,357,913N	Z13	13.6
1.4	cross small meadow	10480	385,649E	4,356,964N	Z13	12.2
2.5	Wurtz Ditch footbridge	10400	383,769E	4,356,745N	Z13	11.1
2.7	cross Wurtz Ditch road	10460	383,671E	4,356,562N	Z13	10.9
3.4	cross Lily Lake Road	10350	382,932E	4,356,261N	Z13	10.2
3.5	cross N. Fork West Tennessee Cr	10320	382,809E	4,356,185N	Z13	10.1
3.7	cross West Tennessee Cr	10320	382,825E	4,355,876N	Z13	9.9
4.1	bear right	10360	382,169E	4,355,712N	Z13	9.5
4.9	join jeep road	10760	381,244E	4,355,702N	Z13	8.6
6.7	enter Holy Cross Wilderness	10920	379,060E	4,354,324N	Z13	6.9
6.8	cross stream in Long Gulch	10920	378,774E	4,354,178N	Z13	6.8
7.7	saddle at Porcupine Lakes	11480	378,148E	4,353,381N	Z13	5.9
8.0	cross Porcupine Creek	11300	378,426E	4,353,154N	Z13	5.6
8.3	seasonal spring	11380	378,642E	4,352,943N	Z13	5.3
9.6	bear right at sharp bend	11280	378,890E	4,351,836N	Z13	4.0
10.2	footbridge over stream	11140	378,020E	4,351,243N	Z13	3.4
10.5	side trail to Bear Lake	11120	377,760E	4,350,973N	Z13	3.1
10.9	C w/W from pond	11100	377,200E	4,350,635N	Z13	2.7
11.4	saddle at timberline, C w/no W	11280	376,655E	4,350,577N	Z13	2.2
11.7	small spring	10560	376,350E	4,350,382N	Z13	1.9
12.9	power line, 1st time	10440	375,856E	4,349,690N	Z13	0.7
13.6	ColoradoTrail TH	10040	375,190E	4,349,393N	Z13	0.0

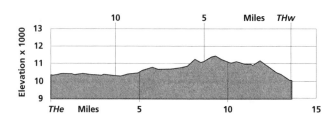

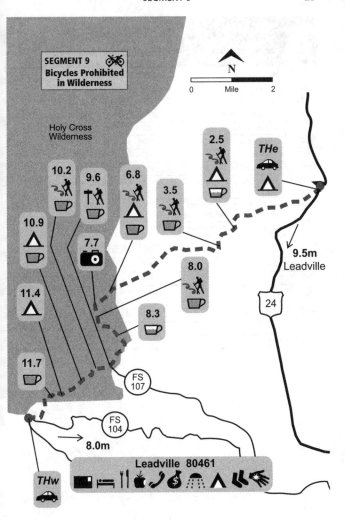

SEGMENT 10
Colorado Trail TH to Halfmoon Creek Rd.
Distance: 13.0 miles   Elevation Gain: approx 1760 ft

`110` `117`

THe	Feature	Elevation	UTM (NAD 83)	THw
0.0	Colorado Trail TH	10040	375,190E 4,349,393N Z13	13.0
1.2	cross bridge	10280	375,857E 4,348,201N Z13	11.8
2.7	unreliable water source	11040	376,682E 4,346,824N Z13	10.3
3.1	Sugarloaf saddle, cross logging road	11080	377,283E 4,346,593N Z13	9.9
3.4	cross small stream	11000	377,088E 4,346,220N Z13	9.6
4.4	cross small runoff stream	10940	377,188E 4,344,911N Z13	8.6
4.9	Twin Mounds saddle, C w/ no W	11000	377,348E 4,344,261N Z13	8.1
5.5	bear to right (old road goes straight), C w/ no W	10600	377,345E 4,343,350N Z13	7.5
6.4	cross Rock Cr bridge, hatchery road (2 m east to old fish hatchery)	10280	377,093E 4,342,766N Z13	6.6
6.7	cross S. Rock Cr on corduroy bridge, potholes in area may have W	10360	377,012E 4,342,367N Z13	6.3
8.0	cross Highline Trail	10960	376,757E 4,340,864N Z13	5.6
9.0	cross North Willow Creek	11040	376,448E 4,339,376N Z13	4.0
9.5	top of ridge, exposed C w/no W	11300	376,650E 4,338,782N Z13	3.5
9.8	side trail to Mt. Massive (3.5 m and + 3,180 ft to summit)	11240	376,720E 4,338,218N Z13	3.2
10.3	cross Willow Creek	11000	376,858E 4,337,696N Z13	2.7
10.8	cross South Willow Creek	10820	376,992E 4,336,884N Z13	2.2
13.0	Halfmoon Creek Road (FS-110)	10080	377,387E 4,334,524N Z13	0.0

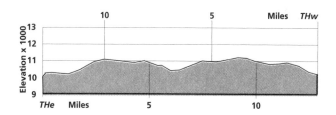

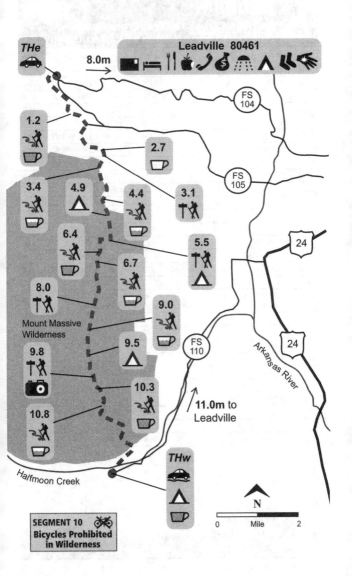

SEGMENT 11
Halfmoon Creek to Clear Creek Road
Distance: 21.5 miles   Elevation Gain: approx 1520 ft

118 125

THe	Feature	Elevation	UTM (NAD 83)	THw
0.0	Halfmoon Creek Road (FS-110)	10080	377,387E 4,334,524N Z13	21.5
1.3	pass side trail to Mt. Elbert	10560	378,312E 4,333,711N Z13	20.2
1.8	cross Box Creek, C 200 ft. south	10440	378,601E 4,333,051N Z13	19.7
2.0	cross Mill Creek	10280	378,856E 4,332,893N Z13	19.5
2.3	intersect and join old road	10280	379,279E 4,332,730N Z13	19.2
2.8	take left fork	10400	379,728E 4,332,038N Z13	18.7
3.1	ford Herrington Creek	10320	379,733E 4,331,555N Z13	18.4
3.8	gain broad saddle	10600	379,876E 4,330,752N Z13	17.7
4.5	pass side trail to Mt. Elbert	10520	379,494E 4,329,841N Z13	17.0
4.8	bridge over stream, join jeep road	10520	379,349E 4,329,432N Z13	16.7
5.3	cross stream	10400	379,763E 4,328,956N Z13	16.2
6.5	leave road, go right	9650	381,612E 4,328,687N Z13	15.0
6.7	pass Lakeview Campground	9560	381,775E 4,328,541N Z13	14.8
7.2	Hwy-82 underpass	9320	381,992E 4,328,038N Z13	13.3
7.8	pass Power Plant Visitor Center	9320	382,867E 4,328,147N Z13	13.7
11.1	turn R off road past bridge – cross marsh	9200	387,780E 4,326,285N Z13	10.4
11.3	C south of river	9200	387,601E 4,326,115N Z13	10.2
13.7	trail junction, take hard left (south) (go west for Hope Pass route in 3.5m or to visit Interlaken site in 1.0m)	9240	384,756E 4,325,965N Z13	7.8
15.0	fork to the left (south)	9820	384,716E 4,325,223N Z13	6.5
15.9	cross seasonal stream	9900	385,337E 4,324,303N Z13	5.6
16.5	cross dirt road	9900	385,728E 4,323,538N Z13	5.0
17.4	go left on dirt road	9800	386,070E 4,322,442N Z13	4.1
17.5	leave road, go right	9780	386,261E 4,322,425N Z13	4.0
18.3	go right on old mine road	9440	386,950E 4,321,971N Z13	3.2
18.9	go right on road, along power line	9360	387,242E 4,321,367N Z13	2.6
20.1	fork left (south)	9760	387,023E 4,320,096N Z13	1.4
20.3	follow jeep rd then trail east along hillside	9760	387,110E 4,319,962N Z13	1.2
21.5	Clear Creek Road	8940	388,944E 4,319,963N Z13	0.0

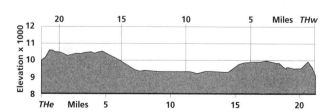

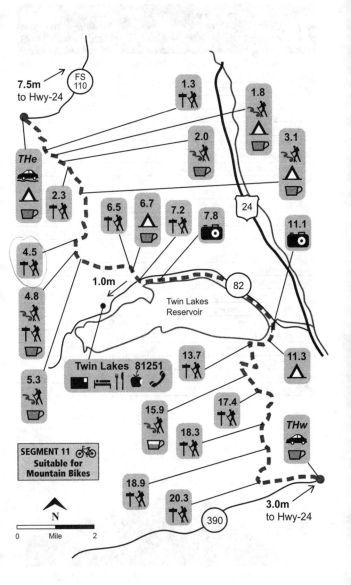

SEGMENT 12
Clear Creek Road to N. Cottonwood Creek
Distance: 18.5 miles Elevation Gain: approx 4520 ft

THe	Feature	Elevation	UTM (NAD 83)	THw
0.0	Clear Creek Road	8940	388,944E 4,319,963N Z13	18.5
0.5	cross Clear Creek on bridge	8950	389,331E 4,319,541N Z13	18.4
1.4	cross power lines	9340	388,825E 4,318,814N Z13	16.9
1.8	cross old road in Columbia Gulch	9640	388,839E 4,318,524N Z13	16.7
3.8	spring, headwaters Columbia Cr	10900	388,425E 4,316,211N Z13	14.7
4.3	spring, headwaters Columbia Cr	11300	388,518E 4,315,444N Z13	14.2
4.8	gain ridge off Waverly Mountain	11640	388,613E 4,314,810N Z13	13.7
6.4	Pine Cr Trail, bridge 500' downstream	10400	389,384E 4,313,657N Z13	12.1
8.1	unmarked trail goes right to Rainbow Lake (0.3m) w/good C and W	11520	389,731E 4,312,397N Z13	10.4
9.0	gain ridge off Mount Harvard	11800	389,867E 4,311,574N Z13	9.5
9.8	cross Morrison Creek	11560	389,916E 4,310,752N Z13	8.7
10.5	cross Wapaca Trail	11500	390,901E 4,310,460N Z13	8.0
11.8	cross Frenchman Cr, w/ Harvard Tr 500' beyond (access for Mt. Harvard and Mt. Columbia via east ridge)	10960	391,074E 4,308,881N Z13	6.7
12.6	gain ridge	11160	392,078E 4,308,530N Z13	5.9
14.2	pass neglected mine and old road	10640	391,944E 4,306,883N Z13	4.3
15.2	cross Three Elk Cr, C 200 ft. south	10280	392,448E 4,305,644N Z13	3.3
15.4	Harvard Lakes, wilderness boundary	10280	392,435E 4,305,356N Z13	3.1
15.7	ford small stream	10160	392,317E 4,304,980N Z13	2.8
15.9	cross Powell Creek	10040	392,331E 4,304,736N Z13	2.6
16.5	cross AU Ranch trail	10000	392,844E 4,304,163N Z13	2.0
17.3	gain ridge	9880	392,320E 4,303,610N Z13	1.2
18.3	right on North Cottonwood Creek Road	9400	392,535E 4,302,469N Z13	0.2
18.5	North Cottonwood Creek Road TH	9400	392,346E 4,302,593N Z13	0.0

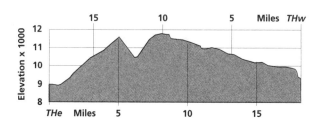

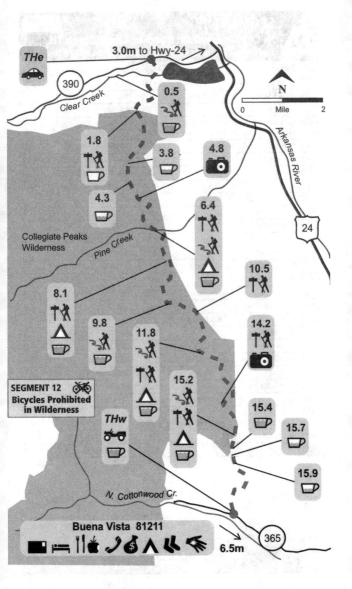

SEGMENT 13
N. Cottonwood Cr. Road to Chalk Creek TH
Distance: 22.8 miles   Elevation Gain: approx 3720 ft

`134` `141`

THe	Feature	Elevation	UTM (NAD 83)	THw
0.0	North Cottonwood Creek Road TH	9400	392,346E 4,302,593N Z13	22.8
2.5	cross Silver Cr, C 0.2m east at ponds	11040	389,394E 4,301,379N Z13	20.3
2.7	wilderness boundary	11200	389,134E 4,301,149N Z13	20.1
3.4	gain saddle on east ridge of Mt. Yale (Mt. Yale side trip: 2m west, with some scrambling)	11880	388,760E 4,300,634N Z13	19.4
4.8	C, W in Hughes Cr down gully west	10640	388,900E 4,298,695N Z13	18.0
6.3	wilderness boundary	9400	389,007E 4,297,155N Z13	16.5
6.5	Avalanche TH	9360	388,786E 4,296,872N Z13	16.3
6.6	cross Chaffee CR-306	9360	388,878E 4,296,794N Z13	16.2
6.7	cross bridge at Middle Cottonwood Cr	9320	388,988E 4,296,693N Z13	16.1
8.8	fork to left where trail splits	9000	391,624E 4,295,488N Z13	14.0
8.9	cross Chaffee CR-344	9000	391,685E 4,295,543N Z13	13.9
9.0	cross bridge at South Cottonwood Cr	8900	391,866E 4,295,419N Z13	13.8
9.5	cross dirt road	8880	392,508E 4,295,787N Z13	13.3
10.5	turn right on road, then fork left in 350'	9440	392,715E 4,295,241N Z13	12.3
11.0	leave road as trail resumes	9560	392,797E 4,294,759N Z13	11.8
11.6	gain saddle west of Bald Mountain	9880	393,425E 4,294,630N Z13	11.2
13.2	cross Silver Prince Creek	9840	394,002E 4,292,735N Z13	9.6
14.0	cross Maxwell Creek, C 300 ft. south	9840	394,537E 4,292,200N Z13	8.8
15.8	cross jeep road	9640	395,870E 4,290,759N Z13	7.0
15.9	bridge over Dry Creek, C 150 ft. south	9600	395,798E 4,290,627N Z13	6.9
17.1	join FS-322 (CT on roads next 5.5m)	9480	396,774E 4,289,482N Z13	5.7
18.2	intersect road into ranch	8960	397,846E 4,288,577N Z13	4.6
18.8	bend to left (north)	8620	398,786E 4,288,499N Z13	4.0
19.1	right (south) on CR-321 (black top)	8550	399,035E 4,288,820N Z13	3.7
20.3	CR-162, turn right (Mount Princeton Hot Springs south across road)	8160	398,830E 4,287,780N Z13	2.5
21.7	veer to left onto CR-291	8300	397,328E 4,286,589N Z13	1.1
22.8	Chalk Creek TH	8360	395,669E 4,286,022N Z13	0.0

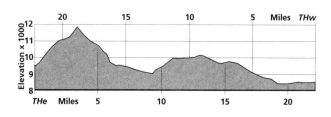

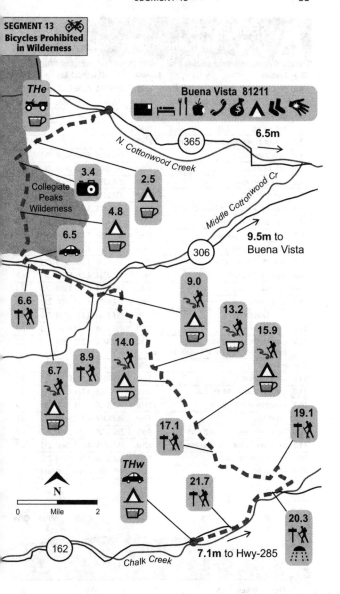

SEGMENT 13 🚲
Bicycles Prohibited in Wilderness

THe

Buena Vista 81211

N. Cottonwood Creek

365   6.5m

3.4

2.5

Collegiate Peaks Wilderness

4.8

Middle Cottonwood Cr

6.5

306   9.5m to Buena Vista

6.6

9.0

13.2

15.9

14.0

6.7   8.9

17.1

19.1

THw

N
0   Mile   2

21.7

20.3

162

Chalk Creek   7.1m to Hwy-285

SEGMENT 14
Chalk Creek Trailhead to US-50
Distance: 20.4 miles   Elevation Gain: approx 3320 ft

`142` `147`

THe	Feature	Elevation	UTM (NAD 83)	THw
0.0	cross bridge south of Chalk Cr TH	8360	395,669E 4,286,022N Z13	20.4
0.1	C left up side trail to Bootleg Campsite	8400	395,719E 4,285,900N Z13	20.3
0.4	cross CR-290	8500	395,932E 4,285,586N Z13	20.1
0.7	fork, go left	8680		19.7
0.9	C, w/small seasonal stream in ravine	8840		19.5
1.4	top out on knoll	9320	396,291E 4,285,071N Z13	19.0
2.1	fork, bear right	9000	397,268E 4,285,280N Z13	18.3
2.2	cross Eddy Creek	9000	397,196E 4,285,103N Z13	18.2
2.4	cross old road	8920	397,202E 4,284,870N Z13	18.0
3.9	cross Raspberry Gulch Road (CO-273)	8960	398,183E 4,282,952N Z13	16.5
4.5	cross eroded jeep trail	9000	398,446E 4,282,224N Z13	15.9
6.1	bear left at trail junction	9720	397,219E 4,280,808N Z13	14.3
6.4	join Browns Creek Trail	9600	397,292E 4,280,441N Z13	14.0
6.6	bear left at trail junction	9640	397,123E 4,280,132N Z13	13.8
6.8	cross Browns Creek	9620	397,277E 4,279,953N Z13	13.6
7.0	cross Wagon Loop trail	9640	397,387E 4,279,866N Z13	13.4
8.7	cross Fourmile Creek	9680	397,062E 4,277,860N Z13	11.7
10.0	cross Sand Creek	9600	397,283E 4,276,298N Z13	10.4
12.2	cross Squaw Creek	9760	396,242E 4,273,962N Z13	8.2
12.7	cross Mount Shavano Trail (side trail to right: 3.5m and +4300 to summit)	9880	395,880E 4,273,299N Z13	7.7
12.9	fork, bear right	9800	395,703E 4,272,954N Z13	7.5
13.2	cross jeep road	9800	395,515E 4,272,626N Z13	7.2
14.9	Angel of Shavano TH, CO-240	9160	393,792E 4,271,443N Z13	5.5
15.2	footbridge over North Fork	9140	393,618E 4,271,144N Z13	5.2
16.7	top of ridge	9760	393,610E 4,270,555N Z13	3.6
18.0	cross Lost Creek, cross jeep road	9400	392,870E 4,269,234N Z13	2.4
19.5	cross Cree Cr, last C north of Hwy-50	9200	391,787E 4,267,794N Z13	0.9
20.2	cross old railroad bed	8880	391,698E 4,267,018N Z13	0.2
20.4	US Hwy-50	8840	391,720E 4,266,827N Z13	0.0

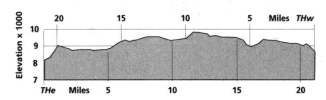

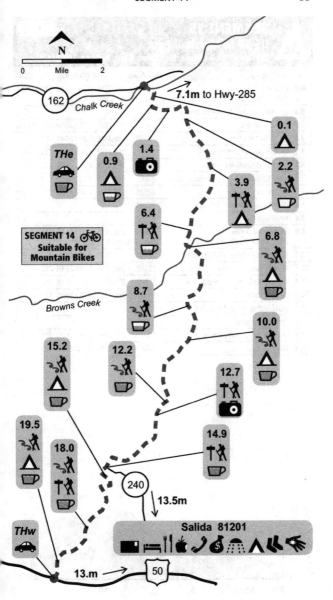

SEGMENT 15
US-50 to Marshall Pass
Distance: 14.3 miles Elevation Gain: approx 3440 ft

`148` `153`

THe	Feature	Elevation	UTM (NAD 83)	THw
0.0	US Hwy-50	8840	391,720E 4,266,827N Z13	14.3
	(hike Fooses Creek Road for next 2.9m, or drive w/high clearance vehicle)			
0.8	reservoir, ample C for next 0.5m south	8960		13.5
2.7	left at road fork	9560	388,764E 4,264,728N Z13	1165
2.8	South Fooses Creek TH	9560	388,788E 4,264,594N Z13	11.5
3.5	footbridge east over Fooses Cr	9720	389,274E 4,263,844N Z13	10.8
4.3	cross S. Fooses Creek west	9840	389,323E 4,262,796N Z13	10.0
5.0	cross S. Fooses Cr east, C north of ford	10169	389,154E 4,261,657N Z13	9.3
5.9	double switchback	10520	388,622E 4,260,550N Z13	8.4
8.1	last W, headwaters of S. Fooses Cr	11240		6.2
8.4	reach tree line	11600		5.9
8.6	Continental Divide	11920	388,578E 4,257,017N Z13	5.7
	(Continental Divide Trail co-locatd with CT next 136m to Elk Cr descent)			
10.3	Green Creek shelter, W 0.3m north	11480	390,165E 4,255,630N Z13	3.9
10.6	re-enter tundra, w/ piped spring	11480	390,317E 4,255,273N Z13	3.7
11.4	cross Agate Creek/Cochetopa Trail	11720	390,458E 4,254,050N Z13	2.9
12.9	join jeep trail	11400	390,299E 4,252,010N Z13	1.4
13.0	piped spring (last W for 12.3m)	11260		1.3
13.6	cross cattle guard	11000		0.7
14.1	Marshall Pass Road (w/toilet pits)	10840	391,045E 4,250,357N Z13	0.2
14.3	Marshall Pass	10880	391,128E 4,250,001N Z13	0.0

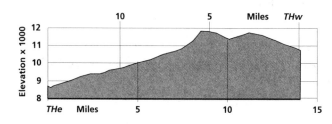

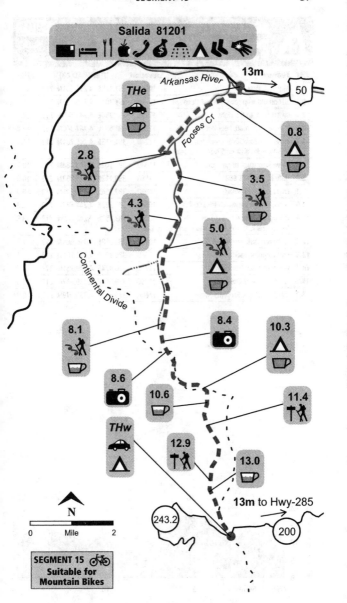

SEGMENT 16
Marshall Pass to Sargents Mesa
Distance: 15.2 miles   Elevation Gain: approx 3080 ft

`154` `159`

THe	Feature	Elevation	UTM (NAD 83)		THw
0.0	Marshall Pass	10880	391,128E 4,250,001N	Z13	15.2
0.2	left on old jeep road, ascend steep hill	10890	391,101E 4,249,957N	Z13	15.0
1.1	switchback to the right	11200	392,250E 4,248,865N	Z13	14.1
2.4	intersect old road, bear left	11160	391,887E 4,247,360N	Z13	12.8
4.1	cross Rainbow/Silver Creek trail, C w/W 0.3m east on Silver Creek Trail	11240	391,513E 4,245,781N	Z13	11.1
4.5	leave jeep track to go right	11440	391,101E 4,245,484N	Z13	10.7
5.2	gate by Point 11,862	11560	390,112E 4,245,353N	Z13	10.0
7.1	cross Jay Creek Road	10880	387,754E 4,245,241N	Z13	8.1
8.9	join gas pipeline swath for 200 ft.	10640	385,322E 4,244,687N	Z13	6.3
11.6	left on old road on west side of Tank Seven Creek, last W for 11 miles until Baldy Lake	10280	383,452E 4,241,460N	Z13	3.6
12.9	Cameron Park, cross FS-578	10800	382,059E 4,240,605N	Z13	2.3
13.8	cross logging road	11080	380,883E 4,240,101N	Z13	1.4
14.1	join jeep track (FS-486)	11240	380,474E 4,240,251N	Z13	1.1
14.7	cross Big Bend Creek Trail	11400	379,958E 4,239,637N	Z13	0.5
15.2	meet FS-855 at Sargents Mesa	11600	379,441E 4,238,979N	Z13	0.0

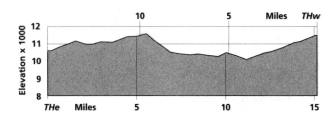

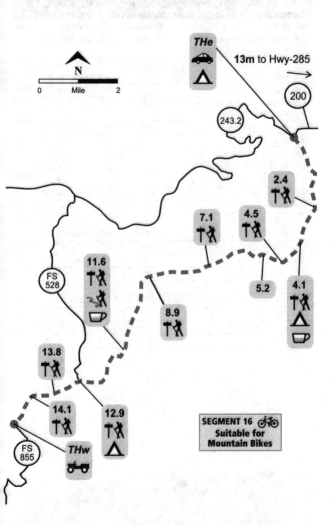

SEGMENT 17
Sargents Mesa to Colorado Hwy-114
Distance: 20.4 miles   Elevation Gain: approx 2440 ft

`160` `165`

THe	Feature	Elevation	UTM (NAD 83)	THw
0.0	meet FS-855 at Sargents Mesa (no W for + 6.9 until Baldy Lake)	11600	379,441E 4,238,979N Z13	20.4
1.0	skirt around north of burned-out knob	11640	378,213E 4,238,210N Z13	19.4
2.3	saddle, go right on poorly marked trail	11160	376,575E 4,238,035N Z13	18.1
2.4	pass Long Branch Trail	11160	376,345E 4,237,950N Z13	18.0
6.9	intersect side trail to Baldy Lake (C and W at Baldy Lake, 0.5m to right)	11480	371,858E 4,241,633N Z13	13.5
7.3	ascend to a high point	11780	371,335E 4,241,664N Z13	13.1
8.4	descend to a saddle	11420	369,708E 4,242,000N Z13	12.0
9.2	reach summit of Middle Baldy	11680	368,575E 4,241,881N Z13	11.2
9.8	pass Dutchman Cr Trail, turn south	11380	367,802E 4,242,074N Z13	10.6
10.0	enter upper part of Upper Razor Park	11216	367,484E 4,241,625N Z13	10.4
10.5	cross Razor Creek	10920	367,273E 4,241,134N Z13	9.9
10.8	bear left, leave creek bed	10880	367,292E 4,240,849N Z13	9.6
12.4	pass side trail to Razor Creek	10960	367,087E 4,238,717N Z13	8.0
14.6	ascend to minor summit	11020	365,587E 4,236,045N Z13	5.8
15.1	descend to forested saddle	10400	365,038E 4,235,610N Z13	5.3
15.5	C w/no W	10500	364,638E 4,235,211N Z13	4.9
16.0	bear left on old logging road	11000	364,001E 4,235,085N Z13	4.4
17.8	bear right on Lujan Creek Road	10320	363,682E 4,233,580N Z13	2.6
18.0	bear left at intersection w/logging road	10320	363,421E 4,233,706N Z13	2.4
19.2	headwaters of Lujan Creek	9840	362,429E 4,233,115N Z13	1.2
20.0	join Hwy-114, go right	9680	361,204E 4,232,024N Z13	0.4
20.4	TH on Hwy-114	9600	360,700E 4,231,743N Z13	0.0

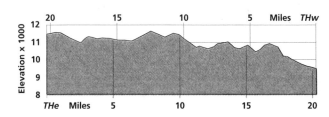

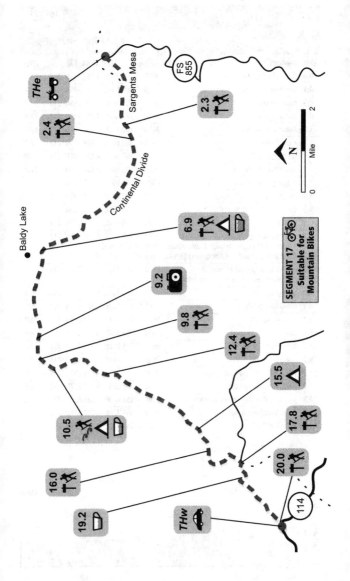

SEGMENT 18
Colorado Hwy-114 to Saguache Park Road
Distance: 13.8 miles   Elevation Gain: approx 1220 ft

THe	Feature	Elevation	UTM (NAD 83)	THw
0.0	Colorado Hwy-114	9600	360,700E 4,231,743N Z13	13.8
0.1	ford Lujan Creek	9560	360,600E 4,231,545N Z13	13.7
0.6	bear to the left	9560	359,973E 4,231,245N Z13	13.2
0.9	join logging road	9560	360,046E 4,230,889N Z13	12.9
1.0	avoid fork to left	9600	360,175E 4,230,731N Z13	12.8
1.7	cross Pine Creek	9680	360,104E 4,229,678N Z13	12.1
1.8	go right at fork	9700	360,083E 4,229,501N Z13	12.0
2.5	switchback to the left	9920	359,648E 4,230,185N Z13	11.3
3.6	logging road ends in cul-de-sac	10000	359,592E 4,228,767N Z13	10.2
3.8	reach saddle, pass through gate	10240	359,441E 4,228,335N Z13	10.0
4.0	go left on logging road (FS-876)	10170	359,368E 4,228,136N Z13	9.8
6.4	pass gate	9780	358,310E 4,225,269N Z13	7.4
6.7	meet Cochetopa Pass Road, follow road to right, through 2 switchbacks. For emergency W, detour to small spring at Luders Campground (3m east on Cochetopa Pass Road.)	9760	358,028E 4,224,952N Z13	7.1
7.2	go left on jeep road, FS-864.2A, cross Archuleta Creek on dirt fill bridge	9620	358,003E 4,224,742N Z13	6.6
8.0	pass gate	9800	357,933E 4,223,755N Z13	5.8
8.3	avoid fork to left	9760	357,527E 4,223,661N Z13	5.5
9.0	turn up the hill	9628	356,417E 4,223,655N Z13	4.8
9.2	sharp right into woods	9666	356,464E 4,223,477N Z13	4.6
9.6	turn down the hill	9619	355,898E 4,223,488N Z13	4.2
9.7	turn to the left	9566	355,763E 4,223,681N Z13	4.1
11.0	reach edge of Cochetopa Park	9400	353,785E 4,223,851N Z13	2.8
11.9	pass gate, fork to right	9360	352,329E 4,223,622N Z13	1.9
12.3	join Saguache Park Road, turn left	9340	352,000E 4,223,820N Z13	1.5
12.9	cross Monchego Creek	9360	351,720E 4,222,911N Z13	0.9
13.8	join FS-787.2D	9520	351,270E 4,221,765N Z13	0.0

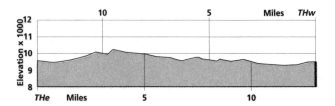

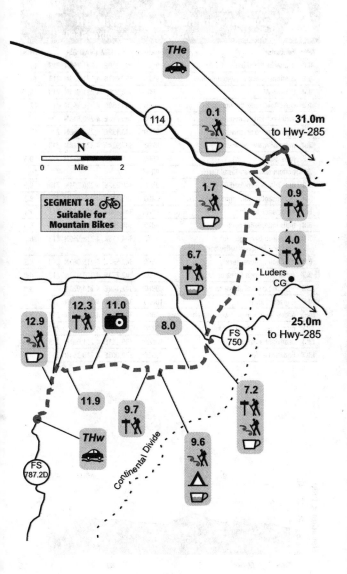

SEGMENT 19
Saguache Park Road to Eddiesville TH
Distance: 13.7 miles Elevation Gain: approx 1660 ft

`172` `177`

THe	Feature	Elevation	UTM (NAD 83)	THw
0.0	Saguache Park Road at FS-787.2D	9520	351,270E 4,221,765N Z13	13.7
0.1	continue straight, avoid right fork	9520	351,057E 4,221,625N Z13	13.6
0.4	C, w/no W	9600	350,995E 4,221,604N Z13	13.3
1.2	cross Ant Creek, through gates	9720	349,589E 4,220,963N Z13	12.5
1.5	avoid left fork, continue west	9760	349,218E 4,220,815N Z13	12.2
2.2	right turn, go northwest	9760	348,138E 4,220,768N Z13	11.5
2.4	maze of roads, go west	9700	347,924E 4,221,028N Z13	11.3
3.2	pass gate	9960	346,842E 4,220,837N Z13	10.5
3.6	bottom out in Van Tassel Gulch	9840		10.1
3.8	turn left on jeep road (FS-597)	9850	346,235E 4,220,294N Z13	9.9
5.4	top of saddle, bear right (FS-597.1A)	10400	345,517E 4,218,032N Z13	8.3
6.6	switchback to left	9960	344,596E 4,218,948N Z13	7.1
6.8	trails intersect at pond	9820	344,260E 4,218,844N Z13	6.9
7.0	leave jeep track, go left (ample C in grassy valley bottom)	9720	344,115E 4,218,569N Z13	6.7
9.5	high point above creek	9960	342,565E 4,215,080N Z13	4.2
9.7	cross Cochetopa Creek on bridge	9900	342,274E 4,214,912N Z13	4.0
9.8	left (SW) on trail above bridge	9960	342,142E 4,214,923N Z13	3.9
10.5	C grassy bench	10000	341,761E 4,214,374N Z13	3.2
10.9	bridge over Nutras Cr wilderness boundary	10000	341,325E 4,213,583N Z13	2.8
12.1	grassy bench above creek	10240	340,016E 4,212,199N Z13	1.6
13.1	bear right at split	10280	339,151E 4,211,061N Z13	0.6
13.7	Eddiesville TH	10320	339,005E 4,210,354N Z13	0.0

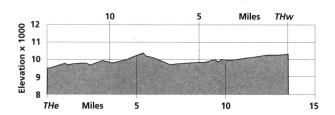

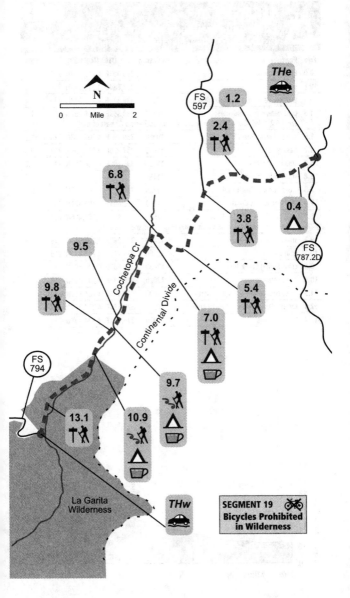

SEGMENT 20
Eddiesville Trailhead to San Luis Pass
Distance: 12.7 miles   Elevation Gain: approx 2960 ft

`178` `183`

THe	Feature	Elevation	UTM (NAD 83)	THw
0.0	Eddiesville TH	10320	339,005E 4,210,354N Z13	12.7
0.1	go left	10340	338,880E 4,210,256N Z13	12.6
0.3	trail leaves road, pass through gate	10350	338,823E 4,210,013N Z13	12.4
1.3	pass gate, enter wilderness	10360	339,553E 4,208,767N Z13	11.4
	(next 6.2 miles: C at numerous spots, W from Cochetopa Cr, east of trail)			
1.6	cross Machin Basin Trail	10360	339,756E 4,208,363N Z13	11.1
3.7	pass gate	10640	337,996E 4,205,956N Z13	9.0
5.5	small side stream	11120	335,499E 4,204,995N Z13	7.2
5.8	small side stream	11180		6.9
7.5	cross Stewart Creek Trail	11720	332,659E 4,204,819N Z13	5.2
7.6	ford Cochetopa Creek	11750	332,604E 4,204,821N Z13	5.1
8.8	gain saddle of San Luis Peak	12600	330,987E 4,204,410N Z13	3.9
	(side trip to San Luis Peak: north along ridge 1.3m and + 1400 ft)			
9.2	small spring	12450	330,995E 4,203,910N Z13	3.5
10.1	gain saddle	12360	329,719E 4,203,859N Z13	2.6
10.5	cross Spring Creek Trail	12080	329,568E 4,203,352N Z13	2.2
10.9	cross small stream	12020	328,934E 4,203,463N Z13	1.8
11.5	cross small stream, begin ascent	12000	328,421E 4,204,113N Z13	1.2
12.1	top the Divide, north of rocky knob	12370	327,680E 4,204,268N Z13	0.6
12.7	San Luis Pass	11920	326,771E 4,204,498N Z13	0.0

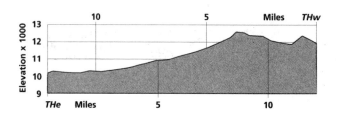

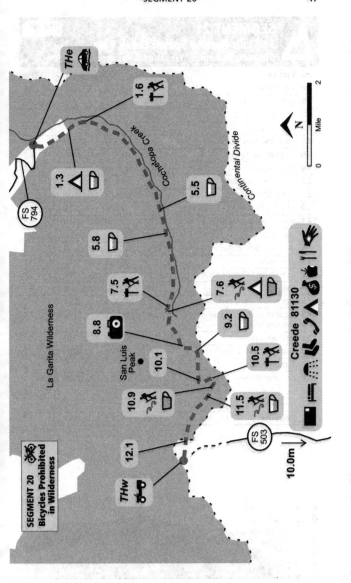

SEGMENT 21
San Luis Pass to Spring Creek Pass
Distance: 14.9 miles   Elevation Gain: approx 2940 ft

`184` `189`

THe	Feature	Elevation	UTM (NAD 83)	THw
0.0	San Luis Pass	11920	326,771E 4,204,498N Z13	14.9
0.3	post, make sharp right and gain ridge	12080		14.6
1.1	base of Point 13111	12760		13.8
1.6	bear left (south)	12250		13.3
2.0	cross tributary of East Mineral Cr	12120	324,927E 4,203,761N Z13	12.9
2.4	campsite, near tree line	12000	324,425E 4,203,802N Z13	12.5
2.6	intersect East Mineral Creek Trail	11840	324,070E 4,203,579N Z13	12.3
2.7	cross East Mineral Creek	11700	323,923E 4,203,649N Z13	12.2
3.3	gain saddle w/post	12160	323,431E 4,203,260N Z13	11.6
4.0	cross Middle Mineral Cr, C 0.1m east	11620	322,627E 4,203,077N Z13	10.9
4.3	intersect Middle Mineral Creek Trail	11480	322,363E 4,203,494N Z13	10.5
4.8	gain saddle	11840	321,838E 4,203,572N Z13	10.1
5.3	avalanche chute, W from snowmelt	12000	321,604E 4,203,060N Z13	9.6
5.7	gain saddle	12240	321,113E 4,202,654N Z13	9.2
6.2	intersect West Mineral Creek Trail	12320	320,568E 4,202,190N Z13	8.7
6.5	gain saddle	12280	320,194E 4,202,346N Z13	8.4
7.6	high point on route, begin descent	12760	319,013E 4,202,624N Z13	7.3
8.3	saddle and intersect Old Skyline Trail, bear left (due south) on CT	12560	317,963E 4,202,880N Z13	6.6
9.5	small pond, turn west	12320	317,755E 4,201,168N Z13	5.4
9.8	cross creek, headwaters Willow Cr	12280	317,385E 4,201,006N Z13	5.1
12.7	final cairn on Snow Mesa	12280		2.2
12.8	post, drop off mesa into drainage	12240	312,771E 4,200,710N Z13	2.1
13.6	tree line, seasonal W in drainage	11640	311,723E 4,201,012N Z13	1.3
13.9	enter stand of spruce, bend to right	11600		1.0
14.9	Spring Creek Pass/CO Hwy-149	10898	310,289E 4,201,367N Z13	0.0

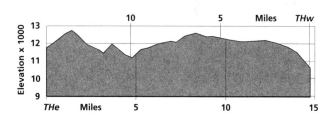

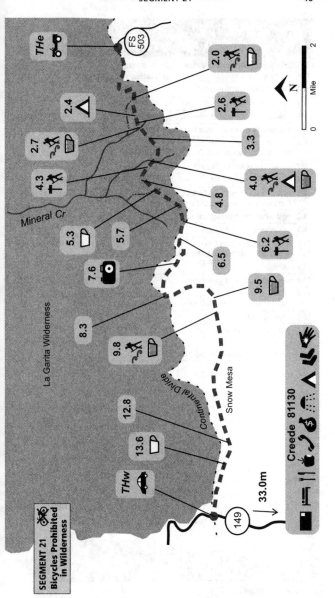

▲ SEGMENT 22
Spring Creek Pass to Carson Saddle
Distance: 17.2 miles   Elevation Gain: approx 3680 ft

`190` `197`

THe	Feature	Elevation	UTM (NAD 83)	THw
0.0	Spring Creek Pass/CO Hwy-149	10898	310,289E 4,201,367N Z13	17.2
1.7	headwaters of Rito Hondo Cr to left	11040		15.5
2.6	bear right off jeep road, cross creek	11320	306,839E 4,200,325N Z13	14.6
4.5	top out near summit of Jarosa Mesa	12000	303,954E 4,200,150N Z13	12.7
5.6	junction with jeep road, go west for C or W, descend to Buck Creek (south)or Rambouillet Park (north)	11700	302,268E 4,200,258N Z13	11.6
6.7	saddle west of Antenna Summit	12040		10.5
7.9	leave jeep track, fork right	12000	299,464E 4,199,593N Z13	9.3
8.7	marshy headwaters for Big Buck Cr, C in trees 0.2m south on CT, W 0.3m east in drainage	11700	298,955E 4,198,584N Z13	8.5
9.2	right on jeep track through willows	12000	299,194E 4,197,912N Z13	8.0
9.5	exit willows, bear left (south)	12200	298,901E 4,197,793N Z13	7.7
11.5	head of cirque for Ruby Creek, W in ponds 0.5m southeast, near tree line	12440	296,757E 4,196,235N Z13	5.7
12.9	saddle	12840	295,610E 4,194,980N Z13	4.3
14.4	saddle, W in pond 0.4m southeast	12840	294,095E 4,193,852N Z13	2.8
15.6	CT highest point (side trip to top of Coney Summit: go northwest 0.2m and + 100 feet)	13271	293,620E 4,192,498N Z133	1.6
16.0	begin big descent	13160	293,263E 4,192,307N Z13	1.2
17.0	go right on intersecting jeep road	12320	293,246E 4,192,308N Z13	0.2
17.2	Carson Saddle (to continue on CT, stay on jeep road, then turn south)	12360	291,701E 4,192,491N Z13	0.0

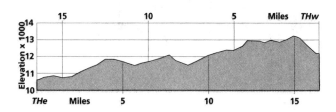

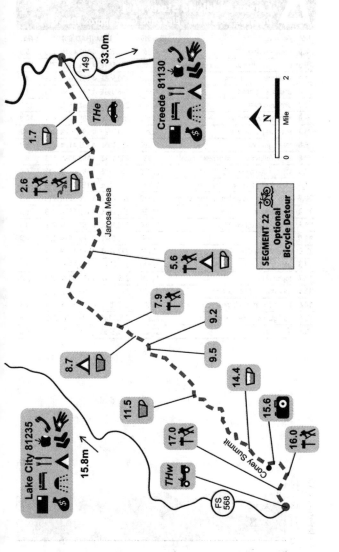

SEGMENT 22
Optional
Bicycle Detour

SEGMENT 23
Carson Saddle to Stony Pass
Distance: 15.9 miles   Elevation Gain: approx 1040 ft

198 203

THe	Feature	Elevation	UTM (NAD 83)	THw
0.0	Carson Saddle	12360	291,701E 4,192,491N Z13	15.9
0.5	bear right off road, C 0.2m southeast	12200	291,567E 4,191,739N Z13	15.4
1.2	small tributary stream	12000	290,598E 4,191,709N Z13	14.7
3.0	double switchback	12560	288,093E 4,192,239N Z13	12.9
3.7	unnamed pass	12920	287,126E 4,192,297N Z13	12.2
5.0	right at trail junction	12360	285,439E 4,191,420N Z13	10.9
5.7	left along small lake	12250	284,782E 4,191,633N Z13	10.2
6.8	take right fork	12670	283,195E 4,191,411N Z13	8.7
7.8	begin following cairns across tundra	12730	282,113E 4,192,070N Z13	8.1
9.3	top of ridge above Cuba Gulch	12720	280,050E 4,191,571N Z13	6.6
9.9	cross trail. Campsite below trail	12540	279,268E 4,191,105N Z13	6.0
10.6	gain saddle and go left at intersection	12910	278,422E 4,190,763N Z13	5.3
11.4	cross Minnie Gulch Trail	12720	278,203E 4,189,553N Z13	4.5
11.6	gain high point on Ridge	12980	278,100E 4,189,155N Z13	4.3
11.9	bear Left	12940	278,052E 4,188,844N Z13	4.0
12.6	cross W Pole Creek Trail	12540	277,777E 4,188,191N Z13	3.3
13.5	pass small pond	12820	277,038E 4,187,096N Z13	2.4
13.7	top of climb	12820	276,771E 4,186,900N Z13	2.2
13.9	go left at trail intersection	12660	276,514E 4,186,805N Z13	2.0
14.6	bear right at trail intersection	12320	276,984E 4,185,969N Z13	1.3
15.5	go right on Stony Pass road	12370	276,114E 4,185,742N Z13	0.4
15.9	Stony Pass	12520	275,826E 4,186,057N Z13	0.0

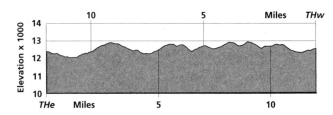

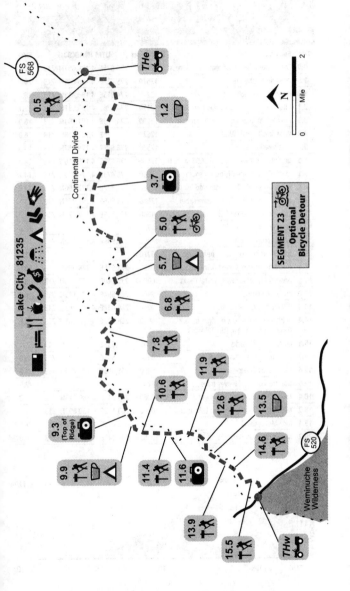

SEGMENT 24
Stony Pass to Molas Pass
Distance: 20.2 miles   Elevation Gain: approx 4460 ft

`204` `211`

THe	Feature	Elevation	UTM (NAD 83)		THw
0.0	Leave Stony Pass road, enter wilderness	12520	275,826E 4,186,057N	Z13	20.2
1.0	cross small stream	12520	275,222E 4,185,046N	Z13	20.1
1.8	cross trail to Highland Mary Lake	12210	274,915E 4,183,818N	Z13	18.4
2.1	hit 2nd trail to H. Mary Lake, turn south	12150	274,678E 4,183,531N	Z13	18.1
3.3	bear left at intersection with side trail	12600	274,759E 4,181,793N	Z13	16.9
4.2	W at small ponds W of trail	12620	275,150E 4,180,478N	Z13	16.0
5.3	C at small lakes	12520	275,888E 4,179,087N	Z13	14.9
5.5	go right (southwest) at fork. CDT splits N	12550	276,855E 4,178,416N	Z13	14.7
6.1	reach Continental Divide, go south	12660	276,473E 4,178,019N	Z13	14.1
6.4	leave Divide, descend right into Elk Cr	12680	276,472E 4,177,596N	Z13	13.8
7.2	headwaters of Elk Creek, mine cabin	12080	275,856E 4,177,471N	Z13	13.2
7.4	cross to south side of Elk Creek	11800	275,535E 4,177,423N	Z13	12.8
7.6	cross to north side of Elk Creek	11720			12.6
8.3	enter spruce forest	11400	274,985E 4,177,528N	Z13	11.9
9.0	trail levels out, several C next mile	10720			11.2
9.6	ford side stream, C next 0.5m	10320	272,915E 4,178,599N	Z13	10.6
11.6	pond, views of Arrow & Vestal Peaks	10000	270,110E 4,178,016N	Z13	8.6
12.0	cross side stream	9960	269,594E 4,178,145N	Z13	8.2
14.3	C w/W nearby, left of trail	9060	266,432E 4,178,763N	Z13	5.9
14.4	wilderness boundary, go right at fork (take left fork to Elk Park RR stop)	9040	266,337E 4,178,801N	Z13	5.8
15.1	cross railroad tracks	8940	265,638E 4,179,411N	Z13	5.1
15.2	cross bridge over Animas River	8920	265,505E 4,179,581N	Z13	5.0
15.4	ford Molas Creek	8950	265,466E 4,179,759N	Z13	4.8
17.6	trail tops out and leaves trees	10280			2.6
18.4	take left fork as trail levels out	10360	263,345E 4,180,415N	Z13	1.8
18.7	take left fork (r. fork Molas Lake 0.2m)	10600	263,152E 4,180,893N	Z13	1.5
19.1	ford Molas Creek	10520	262,839E 4,180,625N	Z13	1.1
20.2	Molas Pass/ US Hwy-550	10880	262,245E 4,180,344N	Z13	0.0

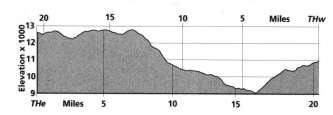

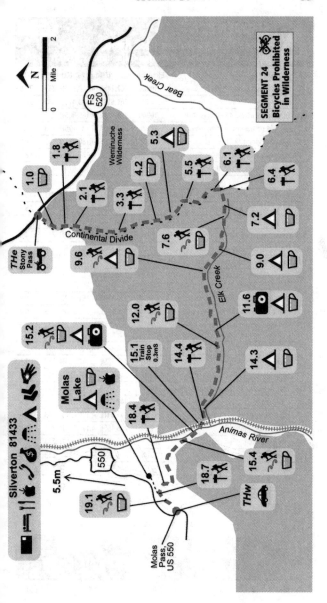

SEGMENT 25
Molas Pass to Bolam Pass Road
Distance: 20.9 miles   Elevation Gain: approx 3120 ft

`212` `219`

THe	Feature	Elevation	UTM (NAD 83)	THw
0.0	Molas Pass/ US Hwy-550	10880	262,245E 4,180,344N Z13	20.9
0.3	power lines	10880	261,873E 4,180,419N Z13	20.6
0.7	cross side trail to Little Molas Lake	10940	261,312E 4,180,606N Z13	20.2
1.5	go right on the intersecting old road	11120	260,785E 4,181,175N Z13	19.4
1.9	seasonal spring	11160	260,229E 4,180,921N Z13	19.0
2.0	leave old road, go northeast	11240	260,128E 4,180,933N Z13	18.9
3.0	join singletrack, go northwest	11560	260,414E 4,181,971N Z13	17.9
3.9	gain saddle	11480		17.0
5.0	viewpoint, C w/W at ponds 0.2m south	11520	258,444E 4,182,867N Z13	15.9
5.3	cross Lime Creek tributary	11500	258,281E 4,183,308N Z13	15.6
5.7	campsite	11500		15.2
6.1	cross upper Lime Creek	11340	257,366E 4,183,709N Z13	14.8
8.0	C w/W 0.1m West	11600	255,388E 4,183,334N Z13	12.9
9.6	spring, then small lake on right	11920		11.3
10.2	meet Engineer Mountain Trail, go right W at nearby lakes, 0.1m north and south of trail	12120	252,838E 4,181,383N Z13	10.7
11.0	join Rico-Silverton Trail, go southwest	12320	251,950E 4,181,899N Z13	9.9
11.2	gain pass, south of Rolling Mountain	12490	251,843E 4,181,740N Z13	9.7
12.3	trail intersection, bear downhill to left (side trail to right leads to C at lake in 0.2m)	11640		8.6
12.9	intersect White Cr Trail, go right (west)	11500	250,381E 4,180,897N Z13	8.0
13.4	crossing of White Creek cascades	10920	249,735E 4,180,795N Z13	7.5
14.7	cross Cascade Creek bridge	10800	249,046E 4,181,555N Z13	6.2
15.5	intersect Cascade Cr Trail, bear right	10840	248,665E 4,180,488N Z13	5.4
17.0	cross stream	11180	247,419E 4,179,726N Z13	3.9
17.3	intersect side trail to FS-579	11280	247,641E 4,179,279N Z13	3.6
19.1	cross saddle	11760	246,169E 4,177,932N Z13	1.8
20.1	turn left on road (FS-578B)	11300	245,102E 4,178,509N Z13	0.8
20.7	leave road, go left on trail	11140	244,274E 4,178,139N Z13	0.2
20.9	Bolam Pass Road/FS-578	11120	244,068E 4,177,965N Z13	0.0

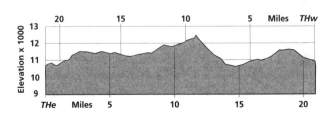

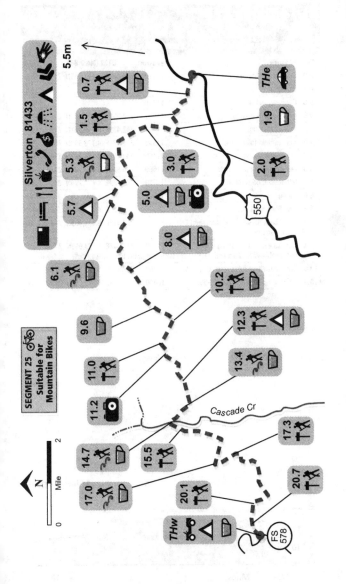

SEGMENT 26
Bolam Pass Road to Hotel Draw Road
Distance: 10.9 miles   Elevation Gain: approx 1480 ft

`220` `225`

THe	Feature	Elevation	UTM (NAD 83)	THw
0.0	Bolam Pass Road/FS-578	11120	244,068E 4,177,965N Z13	10.9
0.1	spring	11120		10.8
0.6	C w/seasonal W	11400		10.3
0.9	gain flat spot on ridge	11520	242,958E 4,177,837N Z13	10.0
1.3	seasonal spring	11500	242,489E 4,178,022N Z13	9.6
1.6	turn left and follow road	11540	242,181E 4,178,337N Z13	9.3
1.7	headwater springs	11460	242,005E 4,178,249N Z13	9.2
3.0	leave road on trail to right	11560	240,516E 4,177,285N Z13	7.9
4.1	left at split, go southwest	11750	239,089E 4,177,294N Z13	6.8
6.6	spring	11700		4.3
6.9	gain Blackhawk Pass	11970	237,186E 4,174,993N Z13	4.0
7.5	switchback to west side of Straight Cr, C 0.1m south	11500	237,433E 4,174,469N Z13	3.4
8.4	cross to east side of Straight Creek, last reliable W for 20m until Taylor Lake (side trail uphill to view waterfall)	10980	237,642E 4,173,999N Z13	2.5
10.0	join old road on ridge crest, C w/no W	10700	238,774E 4,172,374N Z13	0.9
10.9	50' N of Hotel Draw Road/FS-550	10400	239,125E 4,171,049N Z13	0.0

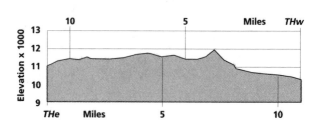

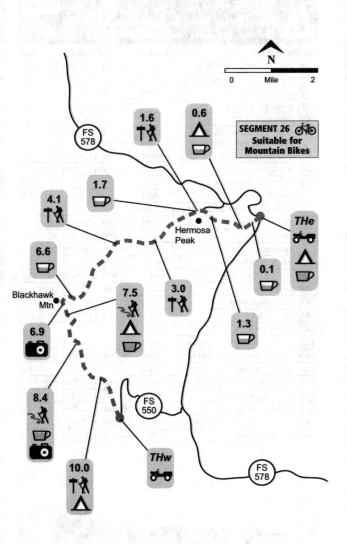

SEGMENT 27
Hotel Draw Road to Kennebec Trailhead
Distance: 20.6 miles   Elevation Gain: approx 3640 ft

226 233

THe	Feature	Elevation	UTM (NAD 83)	THw
0.0	50' N of Hotel Draw Road/FS-550	10400	239,125E 4,171,049N Z13	20.6
0.1	go right on old logging road	10400	239,091E 4,170,948N Z13	20.5
0.6	take side road left	10400	238,476E 4,170,721N Z13	20.0
1.2	go right (west) on trail	10440	238,460E 4,170,120N Z13	19.4
1.3	join road (FS-550)	10440	238,305E 4,170,112N Z13	19.3
1.4	go left at intersection with FS-564, seasonal seep several hundred feet west-northwest of intersection	10440	238,201E 4,170,085N Z13	19.2
1.5	leave road, take trail left	10450	238,134E 4,170,006N Z13	19.1
2.9	pass Corral Draw Trail	10840	237,013E 4,168,800N Z13	17.7
3.4	meet FS-564, then cross it twice more	10760		17.2
4.7	rejoin FS-564	10720		15.9
	NOTE: UTM change to Zone 12 begins below.			
5.0	leave road for trail to the left	10700	764,399E 4,166,626N Z12	15.6
5.6	rejoin FS-564	10700	763,838E 4,166,241N Z12	15.0
5.7	leave road for trail to the left	10720	763,767E 4,166,200N Z12	14.9
6.5	pass Big Bend Trail	10600	763,576E 4,165,143N Z12	14.1
7.1	go left on logging road	10800	762,897E 4,164,601N Z12	13.5
7.9	pass Salt Creek Trail	10840	763,298E 4,163,430N Z12	12.7
8.1	join old logging road	10870	763,151E 4,163,210N Z12	12.5
8.8	take right fork	10880	763,222E 4,162,143N Z12	11.8
11.7	seasonal seeps, C in field to left	11000		8.9
12.3	bench, side trail right for views and C	11320	762,217E 4,158,197N Z12	8.3
13.0	pass Good Hope and Flag Point Trails	11600	762,053E 4,157,856N Z12	7.6
14.1	faint side trail right to seasonal springs	11500		6.5
15.2	intersect Grindstone Trail, go left	11600	761,759E 4,154,954N Z12	5.4
18.3	reach high point on ridge	12300	762,350E 4,150,637N Z12	2.3
18.7	reach a second summit	12260	762,248E 4,150,090N Z12	1.9
19.4	left for CT, go right for Taylor Lake	11640	762,709E 4,149,685N Z12	1.2
20.6	Kennebec Trailhead	11600	764,382E 4,149,157N Z12	0.0

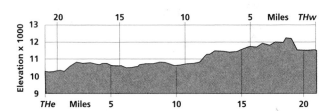

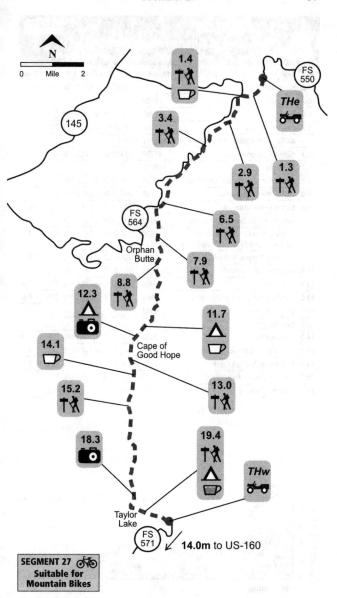

SEGMENT 28
Kennebec Trailhead to Junction Creek TH
Distance: 21.5 miles · Elevation Gain: approx 1400 ft

`234` `241`

THe	Feature	Elevation	UTM (NAD 83)	THw
0.0	Kennebec Trailhead	11600	764,382E 4,149,157N Z12	21.5
0.3	seasonal springs	11680		21.2
0.4	Kennebec Pass	11750	764,995E 4,148,913N Z12	21.1
0.7	turn left off road	11760	765,209E 4,148,699N Z12	20.8
	NOTE: UTM change back to Zone 13 begins below.			
1.1	sliderock traverse, use care	11370	234,955E 4,148,781N Z13	20.4
1.3	tree line	11000		20.2
2.4	cross Champion Venture Mine Road	10340	236,016E 4,149,026N Z13	19.1
4.0	confluence of Flagler Fork	9800	237,154E 4,148,558N Z13	17.5
5.4	Gaines Gulch, waterfall	9140	237,369E 4,147,064N Z13	16.1
5.7	cross to west side of Flagler Creek	9020	237,102E 4,147,083N Z13	15.8
7.1	bridge over upper Junction Creek (W scarce next 11.8m, C in Walls Gulch west of bridge)	8520	236,896E 4,145,211N Z13	14.4
8.4	Road End Canyon, trail follows old road	9440	236,916E 4,143,805N Z13	12.1
11.2	trail tops out, C w/no W	9600	237,868E 4,141,920N Z13	10.3
14.4	pass red gate	8600	236,420E 4,138,600N Z13	7.1
14.6	trail leaves road, left at Dry Fork	8600	236,793E 4,138,500N Z13	6.9
14.8	pass 2nd gate	8580		6.7
15.8	pass 3rd gate	8500		5.7
17.2	cross Hoffheins Trail	8000	240,015E 4,137,998N Z13	4.3
17.4	Gudy's Rest overlook	8020	240,329E 4,138,070N Z13	4.1
18.9	bridge over Junction Creek	7390	240,682E 4,138,256N Z13	2.6
20.3	trail junction, continue straight	7220	241,314E 4,136,340N Z13	1.2
21.5	Junction Creek TH	6960	242,827E 4,135,585N Z13	0.0

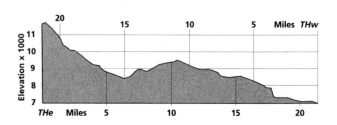

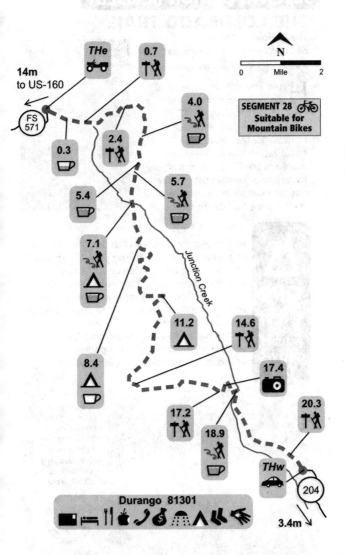

N

0   Mile   2

SEGMENT 28
Suitable for
Mountain Bikes

THe

0.7

14m
to US-160

FS
571

0.3

2.4

4.0

5.4

5.7

7.1

11.2

14.6

8.4

17.4

17.2

20.3

18.9

THw

204

3.4m

Junction Creek

Durango 81301

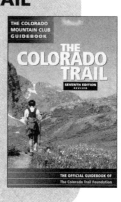